Book 2
Title: "Roots of Resilience: Nurturing Change"

Roots of Resilience: Nurturing Change

The Impact Chronicles, Volume 2

Paul Smith

Published by Paul Smith, 2024.

While every precaution has been taken in the preparation of this book, the publisher assumes no responsibility for errors or omissions, or for damages resulting from the use of the information contained herein.

ROOTS OF RESILIENCE: NURTURING CHANGE

First edition. February 23, 2024.

ISBN: 979-8224630714

Written by Paul Smith.

Table of Contents

Book 2 Roots of Resilience Nurturing Change

SUMMARY:

In the **second** instalment of the **"Impact Chronicles"** series, titled **"Roots of Resilience: Nurturing Change,"**

we follow the journey of a family as they embark on a new adventure in the coastal town of Ramsey. Seeking to break free from the confines of modern technology and reconnect with the natural world, they make the

bold decision to leave behind the hustle and bustle of city life in search of a simpler,

more meaningful existence.

However, their transition to life in Ramsey is not without its challenges. The cost of

moving and the burden of debt weigh heavily on the family, and they soon find

themselves struggling to make ends meet in the face of a growing cost of living

crisis. They face obstacles and setbacks along the way, including financial struggles

and the scarcity of resources, the family finds strength in their resilience and the

unwavering support of the community. Together, they work tirelessly to bring their

vision to life, turning their adversity into an opportunity for growth and

Transformation.

"Roots of Resilience: Nurturing Change" is a poignant tale of perseverance,
community, and the enduring power of hope. It celebrates the resilience of the
human spirit in the face of adversity and reminds us of the importance of staying
true to our dreams, even in the darkest of times.

Book 2 Roots of Resilience Nurturing Change

Chapter 1: A New Beginning

The crisp sea air filled their lungs as the family stepped off the ferry onto the shores

of Ramsey. For Adam, Emily, and their children, it was a moment filled with both

excitement and apprehension. Leaving behind the bustling city life, they embraced

the promise of a fresh start in this quaint coastal town.

As they navigated the narrow streets lined with charming cottages and bustling

shops, they couldn't help but feel a sense of wonder at the natural beauty that

surrounded them. The rugged coastline, with its towering cliffs and crashing waves,

seemed to whisper tales of adventure and possibility.

With hopeful hearts and eager minds, they made their way to their new home, a cozy

cottage nestled among the rolling hills overlooking the sea. As they unpacked their

belongings and settled into their new surroundings, they couldn't help but feel a

sense of anticipation for the adventures that lay ahead.

Little did they know, their journey in Ramsey was just beginning, and the challenges

and triumphs that awaited them would shape their lives in ways they never imagined.

Chapter 2: Settling In

With each passing day, the family found themselves gradually settling into their new
life in Ramsey. The once unfamiliar streets now felt like home as they became
acquainted with their neighbours and the rhythm of the town.
Adam and Emily wasted no time immersing themselves in the community, eager to
make connections and contribute in any way they could. Whether it was volunteering
at the local school or attending town meetings, they were determined to become
active participants in the life of Ramsey.
Meanwhile, the children eagerly explored their new surroundings, discovering hidden
coves along the coastline and making friends at the nearby playground. Their
laughter echoed through the streets as they revealed in the freedom and adventure
that Ramsey had to offer.
As the days turned into weeks, the family's cottage began to feel more like a home,
filled with warmth and laughter. Though challenges still lay ahead, they faced them
with optimism and determination, knowing that together, they could overcome

anything that came their way.

Chapter 3: The Challenges of Change

As the initial excitement of their move to Ramsey began to wane, the family

encountered the inevitable challenges that accompanied such a significant change.

The reality of their financial situation weighed heavily on their minds as they grappled

with the cost of living in their new home.

Adam and Emily found themselves facing unexpected expenses, from the rising cost

of utilities to the high price of groceries at the local market. Each bill that arrived in

the mail served as a reminder of the financial strain they were under, and they knew

they would need to find a way to make ends meet.

Despite their best efforts to cut costs and budget wisely, the family found

themselves stretched thin as they struggled to cover their basic needs. The stress of

their financial situation began to take its toll, testing their resilience and resolve in

ways they hadn't anticipated.

Yet, amidst the challenges, they refused to lose sight of the reasons they had chosen

to make the move to Ramsey in the first place. With unwavering determination, they resolved to face their difficulties head-on, knowing that with time and perseverance,

they would find a way to overcome them.

Chapter 4: Dreaming of Fish Tanks

Amidst the challenges they faced, Adam found solace in his lifelong passion for
marine life. As he gazed out at the expansive ocean from the shores of Ramsey, he
couldn't shake the vision of vibrant fish swimming gracefully in intricate tanks, their
colours shimmering in the sunlight.

With each passing day, Adam's dreams of owning his own fish tanks grew more vivid
and compelling. He spent hours researching different species of fish, studying tank
designs, and envisioning the perfect aquatic ecosystem.

Meanwhile, Emily noticed the spark of excitement in Adam's eyes whenever he talked
about his dream of owning a fish shop and gallery. She admired his passion and
determination, and she couldn't help but feel a sense of pride in his ambition.

Together, they began to explore the possibility of turning Adam's dream into a reality.

They researched potential locations for the shop, brainstormed ideas for its design,
and discussed the logistics of running a business in Ramsey.

As they delved deeper into their plans, they realised that opening a fish shop and gallery could not only fulfil Adam's lifelong dream but also provide a much-needed

resource for the community. With this newfound sense of purpose driving them

forward, they set out to make their dream a reality, one step at a time.

Chapter 5: Exploring Options

With their dream of opening a fish shop and gallery taking shape, Adam and Emily
embarked on a journey of exploration to determine the best course of action. They
spent countless hours researching potential locations, analysing market trends, and
brainstorming innovative ideas to set their business apart.
Their search took them across Ramsey, from bustling commercial districts to
tranquil seaside locales, as they sought the perfect spot to bring their vision to life.
Each potential location offered its own unique advantages and challenges, and they
carefully weighed their options before making any decisions.
Meanwhile, they reached out to local business owners and community leaders,
seeking advice and guidance on navigating the complexities of starting a new
venture in Ramsey. Their conversations provided valuable insights and perspectives,
helping them refine their plans and identify potential pitfalls to avoid.
As they explored their options, Adam and Emily remained steadfast in their

commitment to creating a business that would not only fulfil their own dreams but

also enrich the lives of the people of Ramsey. With determination and perseverance,

they forged ahead, confident that they were on the path to success.

Chapter 6: Community Connections

As Adam and Emily delved deeper into their plans for the fish shop and gallery, they
recognized the importance of building strong connections within the Ramsey
community. They knew that the success of their venture would rely not only on their
own efforts but also on the support and collaboration of their neighbours and fellow
business owners.

With this in mind, they set out to forge meaningful relationships with the people of
Ramsey. They attended local events and gatherings, introducing themselves to their
neighbours and engaging in conversations about their shared love of the ocean and
marine life.

Their efforts were met with enthusiasm and encouragement from the community, as
residents eagerly embraced the idea of a fish shop and gallery in their town. They
offered words of support and advice, sharing their own experiences and insights to
help Adam and Emily navigate the challenges ahead.

As their network of connections grew, Adam and Emily found themselves inspired by the sense of camaraderie and unity that permeated the town. They realised that they

were not alone in their journey, but rather part of a larger community of individuals

who shared their passion for making Ramsey a better place.

Buoyed by the support of their newfound friends and neighbours, Adam and Emily

felt more confident than ever in their ability to turn their dream into a reality. With the

strength of the community behind them, they knew that anything was possible.

Chapter 7: Taking the Plunge

With their plans solidified and the support of the community behind them, Adam and

Emily made the bold decision to take the plunge and pursue their dream of opening

the fish shop and gallery in Ramsey.

Excitement buzzed in the air as they signed the lease for a charming storefront in the

heart of town, envisioning the vibrant marine displays and interactive exhibits that

would soon fill the space. They worked tirelessly to prepare for the grand opening,

painting walls, installing tanks, and stocking shelves with supplies.

As opening day drew near, nerves mingled with anticipation as Adam and Emily

wondered if their vision would resonate with the people of Ramsey. They poured their

hearts and souls into every aspect of the shop, ensuring that it reflected their

passion for marine life and commitment to sustainability.

Finally, the big day arrived, and the doors of the fish shop and gallery swung open to

reveal a world of wonder and discovery. Residents of Ramsey poured in, drawn by the

colourful displays and lively atmosphere, as Adam and Emily greeted them with smiles and excitement.

The grand opening was a resounding success, with visitors marvelling at the beauty

of the marine life on display and expressing their gratitude for the addition of such a

unique and inspiring space to the community. As Adam and Emily looked around at

the bustling shop and the faces of the people they had come to know and love, they

knew that they had made the right decision in taking the plunge and following their

dreams.

Chapter 8: Building Momentum

With the success of their grand opening, Adam and Emily found themselves swept

up in a wave of momentum as their fish shop and gallery quickly became a beloved

fixture in the Ramsey community.

Word of mouth spread like wildfire as visitors raved about the shop's stunning

displays and educational exhibits, drawing in curious locals and tourists alike. The

shop hummed with activity as customers perused the aisles, marvelling at the array

of colourful fish and aquatic plants on offer.

Meanwhile, Adam and Emily wasted no time in building upon their initial success,

working tirelessly to expand their offerings and further establish their presence in the

community. They hosted workshops and educational events, inviting experts to

share their knowledge and passion for marine life with eager audiences.

Their efforts were met with enthusiasm and appreciation from the community, as

residents of Ramsey embraced the shop as a hub of creativity, learning, and connection. From school field trips to family outings, the fish shop and gallery

quickly became a beloved destination for people of all ages.

As their momentum continued to build, Adam and Emily felt a sense of fulfilment

unlike anything they had ever experienced before. They knew that they were making

a positive impact on the community and the environment, and they were determined

to keep pushing forward, one step at a time.

Chapter 9: Overcoming Obstacles

Despite the initial success of their fish shop and gallery, Adam and Emily soon found

themselves facing a series of unexpected obstacles that threatened to derail their

momentum.

Financial challenges loomed large as the costs of running the business began to

mount. From high overhead expenses to unexpected maintenance costs, they

struggled to keep their heads above water and maintain profitability.

Meanwhile, logistical hurdles posed additional challenges as they navigated the

complexities of sourcing and caring for their diverse array of marine life. From

ensuring optimal water conditions to providing adequate space and enrichment for

their fish, they found themselves stretched thin as they tried to balance the needs of

their business with the demands of daily life.

Yet, despite the challenges they faced, Adam and Emily refused to give up. They drew

strength from their shared vision and unwavering commitment to their dream, and

they worked tirelessly to find creative solutions to each obstacle that stood in their way.

With determination and perseverance, they weathered the storm, emerging stronger

and more resilient than ever before. And as they looked back on the challenges they

had overcome, they realised that each obstacle had only served to strengthen their

bond and solidify their resolve to succeed.

Chapter 10: A Fishy Business

As Adam and Emily navigated the ups and downs of running their fish shop and

gallery, they began to realise the true depth of their passion for marine life and the

impact their business could have on the community.

They expanded their offerings to include a wide variety of fish, coral, and aquatic

plants, catering to the diverse interests and needs of their customers. From rare and

exotic species to common favourites, they curated a collection that appealed to both

seasoned aquarium enthusiasts and curious newcomers alike.

In addition to their retail operations, they also launched educational initiatives aimed

at promoting conservation and sustainability. They partnered with local schools and

community organisations to offer workshops and outreach programs, teaching

people of all ages about the importance of protecting our oceans and aquatic

ecosystems.

Their efforts did not go unnoticed, and soon the fish shop and gallery became known

not only as a place to buy fish but also as a centre for education and advocacy.

Customers flocked to the shop not only to purchase supplies but also to learn from

Adam and Emily's expertise and passion for marine life.

As their business continued to thrive, Adam and Emily felt a profound sense of

fulfilment knowing that they were making a positive impact on the community and

the environment. With each new day, they were reminded of the power of following

your passion and the joy that comes from sharing it with others.

Chapter 11: Tides of Change

Just as Adam and Emily were hitting their stride with their fish shop and gallery, a
new challenge emerged that threatened to disrupt their business and test their
resilience: a sudden shift in the tide of consumer preferences.

With the rise of online shopping and changing consumer habits, foot traffic to their
shop began to decline, leaving Adam and Emily grappling with dwindling sales and
mounting uncertainty about the future of their business.

Faced with this unexpected downturn, they knew they needed to adapt quickly to
stay afloat. They brainstormed ideas for attracting customers and increasing
engagement, from hosting special events to revamping their online presence and
exploring new marketing strategies.

At the same time, they leaned on their community for support, reaching out to loyal
customers and local businesses for guidance and encouragement. Together, they
brainstormed creative solutions and rallied around Adam and Emily, determined to
help them weather the storm.

As they navigated the tides of change, Adam and Emily remained steadfast in their

commitment to their dream, refusing to let adversity dampen their spirits. With

determination and resilience, they rode out the rough waters, confident that brighter

days lay ahead.

Chapter 12: Weathering the Storm

As Adam and Emily faced the challenges brought on by shifting consumer

preferences, they found themselves in the midst of a metaphorical storm. Sales

continued to decline, and the future of their fish shop and gallery hung in the balance.

Yet, like seasoned sailors navigating rough seas, Adam and Emily refused to

abandon ship. Instead, they banded together, drawing strength from each other and

their shared vision for the business.

They implemented cost-cutting measures and streamlined operations wherever

possible, finding creative ways to stretch their resources and weather the financial

storm. They also doubled down on their efforts to connect with their community,

hosting events and reaching out to customers both online and offline.

Despite their best efforts, the storm raged on, and there were moments when Adam

and Emily questioned whether they would make it through. But just when it seemed

like all hope was lost, a ray of sunshine broke through the clouds.

Through perseverance and determination, Adam and Emily began to see signs of

improvement. Slowly but surely, sales started to pick up, and the tide began to turn in

their favour.

As they emerged from the storm stronger and more resilient than ever before, Adam

and Emily knew that they had weathered the toughest of challenges and come out on

the other side. With a renewed sense of purpose and determination, they set their

sights on brighter horizons, ready to face whatever challenges lay ahead.

Chapter 13: A Beacon of Hope

After weathering the storm and emerging stronger on the other side, Adam and
Emily's fish shop and gallery transformed into a beacon of hope for the Ramsey
community.

Their perseverance in the face of adversity inspired others, serving as a reminder of
the resilience of the human spirit. Customers returned to their shop with renewed
enthusiasm, drawn not only by the vibrant marine displays but also by the story of
Adam and Emily's journey.

Word spread throughout Ramsey and beyond, and soon, the fish shop and gallery
became known as more than just a place to buy fish—it became a symbol of hope
and perseverance in the face of adversity.

Adam and Emily continued to innovate and expand their offerings, introducing new
products and services that further solidified their reputation as leaders in the marine
industry. From educational workshops to community outreach programs, they
sought to empower others to share in their passion for marine life and environmental

conservation.

As the years passed, Adam and Emily's fish shop and gallery flourished, becoming an

integral part of the fabric of the Ramsey community. Their story served as a

testament to the power of perseverance, determination, and the belief that even in

the darkest of times, there is always hope for a brighter future.

Chapter 14: Rebuilding Together

As Adam and Emily's fish shop and gallery continued to thrive, they felt a deep sense

of gratitude towards the Ramsey community that had supported them through thick

and thin. They knew that they owed their success not only to their own hard work and

determination but also to the unwavering support of their neighbours and friends.

With this in mind, Adam and Emily sought out ways to give back to the community

that had given them so much. They organised charity events and fundraisers,

donating a portion of their proceeds to local causes and organisations in need.

One such initiative involved partnering with local schools to create educational

programs aimed at promoting marine conservation and environmental stewardship

among young people. Through hands-on activities and interactive learning

experiences, they hoped to inspire the next generation to care for the oceans and the

creatures that call them home.

In addition to their philanthropic efforts, Adam and Emily also volunteered their time and expertise to help with community projects and initiatives aimed at improving the

quality of life for residents of Ramsey. Whether it was participating in beach

cleanups or lending a hand to those in need, they were always eager to do their part

to make their community a better place.

As they worked side by side with their friends and neighbours, Adam and Emily were

reminded of the power of unity and collaboration. Together, they were able to

accomplish great things and make a positive impact on the world around them,

proving that when people come together with a shared vision and a common

purpose, anything is possible.

Chapter 15: Seeds of Resilience

Amidst the ongoing success of their fish shop and gallery, Adam and Emily reflected

on the journey that had brought them to where they were today. They marvelled at

the resilience they had cultivated along the way, recognizing that every challenge

they had faced had only served to strengthen their resolve and deepen their

connection to each other and their community.

As they looked back on the trials and tribulations they had overcome—the financial

struggles, the logistical hurdles, the moments of doubt and uncertainty—they

realised that each obstacle had been an opportunity for growth and learning.

They saw how their resilience had not only carried them through the tough times but

had also inspired others to persevere in the face of adversity. They had become

beacons of hope and symbols of resilience, showing that with determination and

perseverance, anything was possible.

With gratitude in their hearts for the support of their community and the lessons learned along the way, Adam and Emily knew that they were prepared to face

whatever challenges the future might hold. They were confident in their ability to

adapt and thrive in an ever-changing world, guided by the seeds of resilience that

they had been planted and nurtured over the years.

Chapter 16: Nurturing Dreams

As Adam and Emily continued to build their fish shop and gallery into a thriving

business, they also remained steadfast in their commitment to nurturing their

dreams and aspirations.

They took time to reflect on their journey and the goals they had set for themselves,

recognizing the importance of staying true to their passions and values. With each

passing day, they found new ways to breathe life into their dreams, whether it was

through expanding their product offerings, launching innovative marketing

campaigns, or forging new partnerships within the community.

But beyond the walls of their shop, Adam and Emily also found themselves nurturing

dreams of a different kind—the dreams of their children. They encouraged them to

explore their own interests and passions, fostering a sense of curiosity and wonder

that would serve them well in the years to come.

Together, as a family, they dreamed of a future filled with possibility and opportunity,

where anything was possible with hard work, dedication, and a little bit of luck. And as they worked towards turning their dreams into reality, they knew that they were

building not just a business, but a legacy that would endure for generations to come.

Chapter 17: Finding Strength

In the midst of the daily hustle and bustle of running their fish shop and gallery,

Adam and Emily encountered moments that tested their strength and resilience.

Whether it was dealing with unexpected setbacks or facing personal challenges, they

discovered that true strength lay not in avoiding adversity, but in confronting it

head-on with courage and determination.

During times of uncertainty, they leaned on each other for support, drawing strength

from their shared commitment to their business and their family. Together, they

faced each challenge with a sense of optimism and a belief in their ability to

overcome whatever obstacles stood in their way.

As they navigated the ups and downs of entrepreneurship, Adam and Emily found

solace in the knowledge that they were not alone. They were surrounded by a

community of friends, family, and loyal customers who stood by them through thick

and thin, offering encouragement and support when they needed it most.

Through it all, they discovered that true strength came not from the absence of fear

or hardship, but from the courage to persevere in the face of adversity. And as they

continued on their journey, they vowed to face whatever challenges the future might

hold with the same resilience and determination that had carried them through thus

Far.

Chapter 18: Rising Above

As Adam and Emily confronted the various challenges that came their way, they
found themselves continually striving to rise above adversity.
They embraced a mindset of resilience, refusing to be defined by setbacks or
obstacles. Instead, they approached each challenge as an opportunity for growth
and learning, determined to emerge stronger and more capable than before.
With unwavering determination, Adam and Emily sought out innovative solutions to
the problems they faced, drawing upon their creativity and resourcefulness to find
new paths forward. They refused to be deterred by failure, viewing it not as a sign of
weakness, but as a stepping stone on the journey to success.
Through their perseverance and tenacity, Adam and Emily inspired those around
them to adopt a similar mindset, encouraging others to rise above their own
challenges and strive for greatness. Together, they forged a community bound by a
shared commitment to resilience and determination.
As they continued to navigate the ups and downs of entrepreneurship, Adam and

Emily remained steadfast in their belief that with hard work, perseverance, and a

positive attitude, anything was possible. And with each new obstacle they overcame,

they grew more confident in their ability to rise above adversity and achieve their

dreams.

Chapter 19: Into the Deep

As Adam and Emily delved deeper into their journey of entrepreneurship, they found
themselves exploring uncharted waters and pushing the boundaries of what they
thought possible.

With each passing day, they ventured further into the realm of business ownership,
taking calculated risks and embracing new opportunities for growth and expansion.

They were unafraid to dive headfirst into the unknown, confident in their ability to
navigate the complexities of the business world.

But their journey was not without its challenges. They encountered obstacles along
the way, from financial setbacks to logistical hurdles, that threatened to derail their
progress. Yet, they refused to let these challenges deter them, instead using them as
opportunities to learn and grow.

As they ventured deeper into the world of entrepreneurship, Adam and Emily
discovered hidden treasures and untapped potential waiting to be uncovered. They
forged new partnerships, expanded their network, and explored innovative ways to

differentiate themselves in a competitive market.

With each new challenge they faced, Adam and Emily dove deeper into their passion

for their business, fueled by a sense of purpose and determination to succeed. And

as they charted their course into the unknown, they knew that they were on the brink

of something truly extraordinary.

Chapter 20: Embracing Transformation

As Adam and Emily reached the final chapter of their journey, they found themselves

embracing transformation in all its forms.

They looked back on the trials and triumphs of their entrepreneurial journey with a

sense of gratitude and pride, recognizing how far they had come since the beginning.

They had weathered storms, overcome obstacles, and emerged stronger and more

resilient than ever before.

But their transformation went beyond just their business success. They had grown

personally and professionally, learning valuable lessons along the way about

perseverance, resilience, and the power of determination.

With newfound clarity and perspective, Adam and Emily embraced the opportunities

that lay ahead, eager to continue their journey of growth and self-discovery. They

were unafraid of change, recognizing it as a natural part of life and an opportunity for

renewal and reinvention.

As they looked towards the future, Adam and Emily knew that their journey was far from over. There would be new challenges to face, new obstacles to overcome, and

new adventures to embark upon. But they were ready, armed with the knowledge and

experience gained from their journey thus far.

With hearts full of hope and excitement, Adam and Emily stepped boldly into the next

chapter of their lives, ready to embrace whatever transformations lay ahead. And as

they did, they knew that they would continue to inspire others with their resilience,

determination, and unwavering belief in the power of transformation.

The End -

Roots of Resilience Nurturing Change

Roots of Resilience Nurturing Change

Roots of Resilience Nurturing Change

Coming Soon

In Book 3, "Echoes of Change: Shadows of the Past," Ramsey faces a new challenge

when a devastating storm tests the town's resilience. As old wounds resurface and

tensions rise, the residents must confront the shadows of the past and find the

courage to rebuild and heal together, forging stronger bonds and deeper connections

in the process.

Book 4, "Seeds of Renewal: Love's Everlasting Bloom,"

BOOK 4, "SEEDS OF RENEWAL: Love's Everlasting Bloom," shifts focus to Emily and

Adam as they navigate the complexities of love, loss, and renewal. Through their

journey, they discover that love has the power to heal wounds, ignite passions, and

inspire transformation, reminding them of the enduring hope that lies within each

new beginning.

Through its heartfelt narratives and compelling characters, "The Impact Chronicles"

explores the universal themes of compassion, resilience, and the profound impact of

small acts of kindness and courage. It serves as a testament to the indomitable

human spirit and the infinite possibilities that arise when individuals come together

to create positive change in the world.

Roots of Resilience Nurturing Change

Roots of Resilience Nurturing Change

Roots of Resilience Nurturing Change

Roots of Resilience Nurturing Change

Roots of Resilience Nurturing Change

Roots of Resilience Nurturing Change

Roots of Resilience Nurturing Change

#Woodystanks
Thank you

Roots of Resilience Nurturing Change

Also by Paul Smith

The Impact Chronicles
Seeds of Change: A Journey to Ramsey
Roots of Resilience: Nurturing Change
Roots of Resilience: Nurturing Change
Rising Tide: The Rebirth of Ramsey
Seeds of Renewal: Love's Everlasting Bloom

Watch for more at wix.pbsmith17@wix.com.

About the Author

Paul smith Artist, Aurthor & Designer. Island resident since 1999
Read more at wix.pbsmith17@wix.com.